Virtual Wealth

How to Create Revenue & Amazing Relationships

Cathryn Marshall

with Jennifer Wright

Virtual Wealth Online
Atlanta, Georgia
www.VirtualWealthOnline.com

ISBN 978-1-7374266-0-8 (Paperback)

ISBN 978-1-7374266-1-5 (eBook)

Writer & Consultant: Jennifer Wright

Cover design by: Kristen Lewter

Cover photo by: Angelina McEwen

DEDICATION

To Joyce Rennolds who has been my friend, mentor and teacher... I am so thankful for her support and influence.

We met when we both spoke at the "Total Woman Makeover" event in 2009.

I was so impressed with her professionalism and delivery. I followed her everywhere and took every class I could.

Her classes and consultations changed my life.

—

Joyce,

I am thankful for your wisdom, blessings and the gift of scripting. My heart is broken that you have left this world.

But I can hear you saying "I love you, I am with you, ... Keep Scripting!"

"Miracles happens when you share your vision with others who believe in you, even before you believe in yourself."

Cathryn Marshall

CONTENTS

GETTING STARTED

It is my greatest hope and joy that you will find and create your own wealth and this book may be a catalyst for positive changes in your life. Virtual Wealth is designed to give you the tools and concepts to attain wealth in each and every area of your life. No boundaries and no ceiling, so please... dream big!

This book is a compilation of simple skills and systems entrepreneurs can immediately utilize to attain their designs of more time, money, peace of mind and quality of life.

I have always believed that we have enough resources in this world, just a severe distribution problem. There is enough time, money and energy. Anyone can change their life.

Many entrepreneurs spend their time over-thinking their programs and pricing. They struggle with clients, sales and marketing. When you focus on the value your provide, you can then change your life and the lives of your clients.

Clients are willing to invest in products and programs that promise to improve health, bring better relationships and increase income. My goal is to help you understand what your clients need so you can serve them and grow your business exponentially.

Collectively, we can work to change the lives of others to make this world a better place. Most of us know that we live 90% of our life in our head. The thoughts we construe as truth become our reality.

We can choose to live in peace, joy, bliss and gratitude. May your stream of consciousness (the words that float through your head) be filled with love and happiness. I hope you'll pass along this collection of concepts to others, so they can live with less worry, less stress and in more joy, peace and prosperity.

1 UNDERSTANDING TRUE WEALTH

"Cherish your life. Cherish your health. Cherish your family. Cherish your friends. For these are the things that money can't buy and will define your true wealth"

- Unknown

She was the wealthiest girl in school. At least from my perspective once I got to know her.

One of my earliest recognitions of wealth came through my experiences as a young teen in a small town in upstate New York. There was a girl in my high school, who was wildly popular. She had tons of friends and was voted homecoming queen, almost unanimously.

I vividly remember begrudgingly filling out my voting card and making comments about the entire process being nothing but a popularity contest.

One day, after running into her in the hallway, she invited me to her house. To my 15-year-old self, it felt like such an honor to be chosen to spend time with her. Although it was a long walk across town, I happily made the trek because the most popular girl in school wanted to hang out with me.

When I got to her house, I noticed how small the house was. It was clear her mom was a single mom, and worked really hard and that they lived in a rented home. It was also clear that Kristen and her mom had a very deep connection with each other and a closeness that I wasn't expecting to experience with a fellow high-school student. It was as if her mom's presence, even though she was at work, was telling me that life was beautiful no matter what the circumstances.

Kristen was not at all apologetic or embarrassed by the house or her circumstances. She greeted me with no makeup and in a robe with her hair in a towel. She did not apologize for her appearance. She was just happy to have me over!

I realized that day as we spoke that my self-talk and my statements were self-deprecating. Kristen was so kind to me. She corrected me both with and without words and brought me up to a higher place. She was sweet and complimentary. I left feeling like I had been entertained in a movie star's home. I had a lot to think about.

Kristen was the prettiest and most popular girl in the school. She looked gorgeous every day, carried herself with confidence. She had a lot of friends. I spent one afternoon with her and she changed my life for the better. I was proud to know her. I voted for her.

The Kristen I knew in school was the richest, wealthiest girl in my class. Pretty. Popular. Incredibly well dressed. Carried herself gracefully as she walked down the hall. Happy. Smiling all the time. She was wealthy.

When I was 16, I started running a painting business. For six years I painted homes and commercial businesses. I did everything from the payroll, accounts payable and receivable, managed employees and bid on the jobs.

The skills I learned as a young person of managing employees, paying taxes, accounting, payroll and making money would shape my entire life. I enjoyed the business. From that business, I made enough money to pay cash for a house and I managed the renovations of the house.

Unfortunately, that business would come to an end when my fiancé and I ended our relationship. He had been my business partner and when we decided to not get married, I knew that business would not be my long-term career.

The ending of the relationship as well as the ending of the business led to a near nervous breakdown, panic attacks and months of heartache over the breakup. Going through that pain and anxiety created a great deal of resilience and gave me the ability to handle almost anything that life threw at me after that. It also led me to go on to obtain three college degrees and eventually move to Atlanta and start my own personal training business.

While I worked on my degrees, I worked a number of different jobs in that small town in upstate New York. I taught in a daycare. I worked in a warehouse sorting tomatoes and cucumbers. I cleaned motel rooms. I sold photography services. I tended bar and (my all-time favorite job) I waitressed at Perkins Pancake house (Perkins Restaurant & Bakery).

Through all of those experiences, I learned the value of relationships. I learned that everyone has a story and I learned how to relate to each person through their stories.

Ultimately, I learned that my primary relationships, friendships, health and financial stability were all tied together. My level of happiness, mental and emotional stability and perception of well-being were all tied intricately together.

I built a life much like the one I observed with my high school friend, who was the example of living a wealthy life. I made friends, created a business that brought me personal rewards and built a network of amazing professionals.

Eventually, I began to live in a low-stress, healthy environment within each of the pillars of virtual wealth.

Wealth Concept

My core value is freedom

The small college town where I grew up was a very close-knit community that allowed me the opportunity to have a lot of mentors - at work, school and within my own family.

Education has always been highly valued in my family. My Mother, Grandmother, Great Grandfather and Aunt were all educators. In fact, my grandmother was ahead of her time as one of the earliest paid female educators. She often told me about how only men were teachers when she was younger. She also remembered the great depression and there being no jobs which made it even more extraordinary that she was able to have a job as a teacher.

Even though the importance of school was ingrained in my family, I almost didn't graduate high school. I had poor study habits and apathetic attitude when my parents.

I was actually voted "most absent" my senior year.

Despite barely graduating high school, I went to college to become a therapist and graduated with honors, three times. I quickly learned what I wanted my life to be and I knew education had to be part of that. I grew up quickly with my study skills and attitude. I was driven to get A's all the while working and supporting myself. I was grateful my parents paid my tuition and books so that I could get a higher level of education.

What is Virtual Wealth?

Along the way, I developed an understanding that true wealth means having a completely healthy life in many ways. Essentially wealth is health on many levels. It is happiness. It is contentment. It's also a sense of well-being and whatever you need to feel whole to function and be productive.

Having virtual wealth simply means that you are able to have that same complete life and have a business that you love. Especially now more than ever, "virtual" means no boundaries

Virtual wealth means being able to work and be productive wherever you are or want to be, from anywhere in the world.

Virtual wealth means being able to work with anyone wherever they are and need to be from anywhere in the world.

Virtual wealth means being able to influence, teach and mentor in any way necessary to reach your people.

Virtual wealth means creating the days, weeks, months and years that align with exactly what I want my life to be.

Virtual wealth means creating the space to spend the time with my family, my friends, myself and taking the time to take care of my needs for my own self-care.

Six Pillars That Create Virtual Wealth

The most successful people work on themselves personally to become better in each area of life that they deem needs attention.

1. *Mental Health & Emotional State:* Mind and thought processes

2. *Physical Health:* A healthy, fit body

3. *Social Health & Healthy Relationships*: family, friends, co-workers

4. *Spiritual Health*: Practices and development

5. *Financial Health:* Living Debt Free and having the skill to manage money well

6. *Creative Expression:* The joy that brings each area together

I used to count the SIX CATEGORIES off on my fingers again and again. Six categories that seemed to make sense. My goal was to achieve some sense of focus and improvement in each and create balance and alignment. If I could do that, I would feel better throughout the day. I would surely make better choices and decisions to reap the benefits.

Have you ever imagined waking up in the morning and feeling like you stepped into utopia? What if you woke up and realized upon your first moments of consciousness that you felt incredible, and you had everything you ever wanted in life and more was coming?

I used to wake up afraid. The feeling of being scared was in my belly. Scared I would not be able to make it. Scared I would run out of work. Scared I would run out of money. Scared life would implode upon me. Scared someone was not going to be happy about something, and my name was on the bottom line. The truth was that feeling this was utterly ridiculous based on my actual circumstances.

Once I was able to create the business and the life that I truly wanted, I went from waking up afraid to waking up feeling absolutely amazing, excited for another day, blessed and grateful. This changed my life in every way possible.

I'm going to explain how I did it and every single concept you can put in place in your life to change your thoughts, feelings and actions to manifest virtual wealth for yourself. I promise to use simple terms and give you the steps you can absolutely do. And it's not going to be hard. It's actually going to be fun and easy.

2 YOUR VIRTUAL LIFE BY DESIGN

"Be bold enough to use your voice, brave enough to listen to our heart and strong enough to live the life you've always imagined."

Unknown

Creating wealth is not just about having more money. Wealth can come in the form of time, relationships, family, talents, connection, community, learning, confidence and health (add any number of other items that are important to you).

Creating wealth - in all of its forms - can bring you quality of life.

Creating wealth can help you create freedom - freedom from financial stress, freedom from life stresses and freedom to create the person you want to be.

Creating wealth can allow you to spend more time with your family and more time to do what you want - travel, learn, grow and create. The time you create can help you to improve your health and feel better in your body.

Creating wealth can improve your quality of life and your relationships with your friends, your family and your community.

At the age of 19, I experienced high levels of anxiety and started working with my first therapist. Looking back, I simply wanted to feel better and be more productive. I sought out someone with whom I could connect. During the process, I became fascinated by the prospect of changing a person's mindset to alleviate mental health disorders. That was when I made the choice to follow a similar path.

I decided to become a therapist for two reasons. I wanted to work on my own issues and I had a deep desire to help others.

By being aware of my own challenges and realizing that I had the ability to create the changes that I wanted, I became highly resilient. Mastering resilience would prove to be one of the greatest skills in life that got me through many challenging situations.

Your belief systems help to define who you are. You are a combination of who people told you that you are and you embraced those concepts as a part of your beliefs to form your identity.

My mother told me when I was a little girl "You are a leader, not a follower." Thank you, Mom. Those words shaped my entire life.

We run off of our belief systems. Whether they are positive or negative, our belief systems run our entire life.

In 2008, my business coach, Andy Lowe told me:

"When you begin with the end in mind, you can fill in the pieces of the puzzle as you go"

I worked with Andy to design the perfect schedule, hours, and income. We studied concepts of the laws of mental toughness. We practiced Elevator Speeches and he coached me to be incredibly good at teaching elevator speeches. He asked me several times to come work for his company. I declined several times. I simply wanted to build personal training programs. I wanted to stay in the health and fitness arena and not branch out into business coaching. However, I ended up hiring several coaches and continue to immerse myself in coaching.

When you live your life by design, you literally are calling the things that you want into existence. You come to a place of knowing

Throughout my career, I have created the life that I needed. Many times it was intentional and sometimes it wasn't. When I was 16 and owned the painting business, I created a business that helped me to become independent and it helped support the families of all of my employees.

In 1997, I started my personal training business, had a baby and was in a marriage that was not going to last. I needed to be able to support my son and create independence again for myself. I also had a deep desire to help those who were in pain and struggling to lose weight, get fit and improve their own lives.

In 2018, I left the personal training business and took my business 100% virtual. It was HARD. I felt that I was walking away from my comfort zone. I knew there were bigger opportunities out there for me.

After years being a personal trainer, I realized I was trading dollars for hours which resulted in 60-hour work weeks for many years. I knew that would only take me so far. I also knew that I had the ability to create a bigger life, more freedom, more choices and more relationships.

"Who I am is what I'll get"

I heard the above statement during a virtual coaching session and it struck a chord.

I knew that building a virtual life would help me to achieve my dream of helping 1,000,000 people or more.

This life that I lead now is completely by design and is being designed every day with every new concept, every new relationship and every new client.

It is a life where I learn every day. I take care of myself every day. I meet new people and build new relationships every day.

Building Your Intentional Virtual Life. A Creative Process.

Use the following exercise to help you define what your virtual life will be.

First, let's prepare. You want to find a time and place that helps you to be creative. I recommend setting aside a little time that you can focus on your goals and aspirations. Make sure you have something to write on and something to write with. Choose anything that you like. You can use your favorite journal or notepad or even a whiteboard. I like to write with pencils - both graphite and colored pencils. You can choose colored pens or anything that you like.

I usually put on some focus music (checkout the Focus@Will app) or I ask Alexa to play spa music or meditation music. You may prefer no sound at all. This is all about your creative process.

Once you are prepared and relaxed, take a couple of deep breathes and let's get started.

1. Close your eyes and think about what your perfect day would be like.

   ➢ How do you wake up? What time?

   ➢ What is the first thing you would do after you wake up?

   ➢ Who is there with you?

   ➢ What does the room look like?

   ➢ If you look out your window what do you see?

   ➢ What is on your schedule for the day? Are you seeing clients? Are you spending time with your family or friends? Are you working on your business? Are you practicing self-care?

   ➢ What are you grateful for?

   ➢ How do you feel at the end of the day?

2. Write everything down. Keep writing until you can't think of anything else to write.

3. Close your eyes and imagine all everything that you just wrote down. Imagine yourself doing everything you captured.

4. Think about how it makes you feel.

5. Spend as much time meditating on that image and feelings as you need.

6. When you are finished, open your eyes, look at your list and circle those things that your wrote down that are the most important to you.

This is now the beginning of your goals for your business and your life. These goals will help you to build your plan so that you can achieve exactly what you want.

3 CREATE THE LIFE YOU DESERVE: THE WHEEL OF LIFE

"Before you speak, listen. Before you write, think.

Before you spend, earn. Before you invest, investigate.

Before you criticize, wait. Before you pray, forgive.

Before you quit, try. Before you retire, save.

Before you die, give."

William A. Ward,

Writer and Poet

You can find lessons in a lot of experiences. My son was a toddler in daycare in 2002. The daycare asked me for help with a fundraiser so I did a sponsorship offering my services as a personal trainer. Back then I didn't even know what a sponsorship was.

I wrote the offer up and noticed there was another woman offering life coaching sessions. That was when I met Susan Longley, who became my life coach. Susan introduced me to professional networking and the concept of the Wheel of Life.

Here's how the wheel works: If you were to draw a circle around the lines of the outside of the wheel with one being at the center, and 10 being on the outside, you rate your level of satisfaction and development for the category. If you are on the outside of the circle, you are completely satisfied. If you are at the center, or at a low number, it may be an area that you decide to focus on, get educated and do some personal development work within.

Wealth Concept:

There are an unlimited number of tools in your toolbox. Don't forget you have them.

I've revisited this Wheel of Life exercise yearly and sometimes multiple times per year to check in with how I'm doing. My wheel started out pretty choppy in 2002 and got rounder over the years.

WHEEL OF LIFE

The Wheel of Life is broken down into 7 categories

Health is directly related to how you feel physically and can influence how you feel emotionally. Health is directly related to the food you eat, your activity levels, stress, sleep, chronic conditions and any number of other factors that impact your mind and body.

Spirituality, in all of its forms, helps us to stay grounded. It helps us to maintain a focus outside of ourselves. As we evolve our spiritual practices, we help to build our belief system and manifest what we want to create in our lives. Some of the spiritual practices that can help us to grow include prayer, journaling, meditation, scripting and reading from spiritual contexts.

Family is such a key part of our lives. Family can include our blood relatives or any other people in our lives that we consider to be part of our family. Having balance in our family can impact as much as or more than any other factor on the Wheel of Life although those balanced relationships don't always come easy. Paying specific attention to this area can bring significant improvements to our lives overall.

Travel helps us to not only find ways to relax but to also explore our world. Our overall happiness and health can be benefited by being able to explore other places, learn about those who live different types of lives, learning about other's histories. Travel can also give us an opportunity to disconnect from our very busy lives. It allows us the ability to find fun places for us to relax.

Work is what gives us purpose. Studies have shown that most people want to be able to do work that is fulfilling, purposeful and gives them a sense of accomplishment. Having work that makes you feel good or that you have contributed to someone else's life, can help to make your overall life more exciting and fulfilling.

Money is needed in order to help us fulfill basic needs and help us to support the things that we care the most about – family, education, health, adventure, fun. It can also be a powerful tool in allowing us to help others.

Social interactions speak to our emotional, mental and physical health. Researchers have found that having strong social bonds and support helps to build self-esteem and confidence. Those relationships help to reduce depression. Social networks help us to grow, learn and be more successful in our lives.

Wheel of Life Exercise: Evaluating and Goal Setting

Use the exercise on the following pages to build and assess your Wheel of Life.

I suggest that you find a quiet place to go through this exercise. If you meditate, you might do a short meditation beforehand to help create a peaceful mindset and open yourself up to possibilities. Make sure you have at least 30 minutes to perform the exercise. Spend time really considering what you have in your life and what you want in your life.

Step 1 - What you currently have in your life:

On a Scale of 1-6, indicate where you think you are in achieving your goals in each of these categories

1 = I am not achieving my goals or I have not set any goals

6 = I am exactly where I want to be

1. Health _____

2. Spirituality _____

3. Family _____

4. Travel _____

5. Work _____

6. Money _____

7. Social _____

Now take a marker, crayon, pencil or anything you would like and fill in the wheel with your scores. If you'd like, make a copy of the page so that you can do the exercise again and see how you progress over time.

Step 2:

On the next page, define the goals that you would like to set for yourself for each item. Think about what you would like to have in 1 year, 3 years and 5 years.

Pay close attention to those items that you rated a 3 or less.

	What I want in my life in the next year	What I want in my life in the next 3 years	What I want in my life in the next 5 years
Health			
Spirituality			
Family			
Travel			
Work			
Money			
Social			

These goals that you set for your life can also be used as you start to set goals for your personal business.

For instance: if one of your goals is to travel internationally at least once per year, you can set your business goals around both financially being able to travel internationally as well as ensuring that you have the time in your business to travel.

4 HEALTH IS WEALTH: THE WHEEL OF FITNESS

"If you look at what you have in life, you'll always have more.

If you look at what you don't have in life,

you'll never have enough."

Oprah Winfrey,

Host, Producer and Philanthropist

You have only one body. You must take great care of it to live your best life.

When you prioritize taking care of your body you are better able to take care of you and your clients. Having a healthy, fit body helps to give you more energy. It helps to build your immune system and keep you from getting sick. When you do fall ill, the healthier you are the quicker you are able to recover.

Many times, we get so busy and unfortunately, for many of us, our health is what gets put on the back burner. We set health goals for ourselves and don't fulfill them. We don't have time to prepare healthy snacks or take that walk or get a workout in.

If that sounds like you, don't be upset. You are not alone.

I used to be that person who was "a procrastinator" when it came to workouts and eating well. It just fell off the back end of what was important for the day. I had a lot to do. Life was busy. I had my circumstances to deal with.

When I was 22, I was living with my mother and working in an ice cream factory. We ate a lot of Steve's Ice Cream. With 32% milkfat, it was considered one of the best ice cream brands around. On the production lines, we ate all the ingredients. I remember my grandmother smiling, clasping her hands and asking me, "How much weight have you gained while living at your mother's?" The answer was 15 lbs.

I struggled with sugar addiction, procrastination, and binge eating for years. It was challenging and painful. I entered the fitness industry at the age of 27. I opted in while I was pregnant and made the decision that I was going to be fit and become a leader in the industry. It sounded like a lot more fun than social work. My first job was to get myself in shape. It was then that I created the Wheel of Fitness as a way to understand the important connection between health and fitness and the other elements in my life.

The Wheel of Fitness

Understanding the Wheel of Fitness helps you to identify the areas where you need more attention and to set your health goals. What's great about this exercise is that you can design your fitness goals to fit your life.

WHEEL OF FITNESS

Nutrition is all about what you put in your body. You really are what you eat and the body does well with real food. The only things that are meant to go into our body as the foundation of what we eat are water, protein and vegetables.

Balancing your blood sugar levels by eating quality sources of protein and green vegetables is the foundation of having energy and excellent health.

Cardio is exercise that involves challenging the cardiovascular system. The benefits of cardiovascular exercise are energy, lower body fat percentage and stamina. You must increase your heart rate regularly to improve cardiovascular endurance. Running, biking, walking, swimming, and using cardiovascular equipment are options to get this type of exercise into your daily routine.

Strength Training involves moving your muscles with bodyweight exercises, dumbbells, and strength training machines. The only way you can physiologically increase your metabolism is through consistent strength training.

Flexibility including stretching is incredibly beneficial to help with pain and increases your mobility. Focusing on your flexibility can help you to improve your range of motion, keep your muscles elastic and help to keep your joints moving freely.

Balance is an even distribution of weight that helps to enable you to stay upright. As we age, for many of us, our balance starts to diminish due to a number of factors. Muscle mass decreases, our reaction time decreases, and medications can impair our balance. It is important to focus on joints and muscles that help us to balance and help to ensure that we address anything that could increase our risk of fall.

Alignment involves ensuring that you have symmetry of muscular strength and keeping the bones in the correct position or appropriate relative positions. Ensuring that our skeletal system is aligned can have many benefits. When the skeletal system is aligned, the bones and muscles are working against each other and helping to eliminate pain. Having proper alignment can also improve balance and help ensure that the exercise that we are getting gives us the most benefit possible.

Posture increases both your balance and your strength. Your mother may have told you when you were little to sit up straight or hold your head up when you walk. She was right. Our modern lifestyles don't always promote good posture. Many of us have jobs that require us to sit or stand for long periods of time. Focusing on good posture can have great benefits to your health. It can reduce backpain, reduce headaches, increase your energy and a host of other benefits.

Wheel of Fitness Exercise: Evaluating and Goal Setting

Use the exercise on the following page to build and assess your Wheel of Fitness. (Note: follow the same instructions as the Wheel of Life exercise.)

I suggest that you find a quiet place to go through this exercise. If you meditate, you might do a short meditation beforehand to help create a peaceful mindset and open yourself up to possibilities. Make sure you have at least 30 minutes to perform the exercise in order to help make sure you spend some time really considering what you have in your life and what you want in your life.

Step 1 - What you currently have in your life:

On a Scale of 1-6, indicate where you think you are in achieving your goals in each of these categories

1 = I am not achieving my goals, or I have not set any goals

6 = I am exactly where I want to be

1. Nutrition _____

2. Cardio _____

3. Strength _____

4. Flexibility _____

5. Balance _____

6. Alignment _____

7. Posture _____

Now take a marker, crayon, pencil or anything you would like and fill in the wheel with your scores. If you'd like, make a copy of the page so that you can do the exercise again and see how you progress over time.

Step 2:

On the next page, define the goals that you would like to set for yourself for each item. Think about what you would like to have in 1 year, 3 years and 5 years.

Pay close attention to those items that you rated a 3 or less.

	What I want in my life in the next year	What I want in my life in the next 3 years	What I want in my life in the next 5 years
Nutrition			
Cardio			
Strength			
Flexibility			
Balance			
Alignment			
Posture			

Focus on making your goals achievable. There are lots of ways to ensure you reach your goals and lots of ways to make it easier on yourself.

For example, if one of your goals is to improve your strength, you can design your day to make sure that you have time to do strength exercises by either setting aside time in the morning or evening or even finding time during the day. There are lots of options. You can strengthen your muscles with exercises using your own bodyweight, strength bands, free weights, or go to a facility and workout using the strength machines.

5 DESIGN YOUR BUSINESS: THE WHEEL OF BUSINESS

"Don't be afraid to reach for the stars. To want more out of life is normal. To get more out of life is extraordinary."

George Turmon,

IFBB Pro Bodybuilder

I have business in my blood. My great grandparents owned an electric store when electricity first came out. My uncle owned four businesses. My stepfather's family owns a printing company that is over 100 years old.

Your business needs to feed your soul. Your business also needs to bring you a sense of fulfillment, accomplishment and fill your bank account. If you are lucky enough and have the right business model, your business brings you joy, bliss and happiness. It will do this despite the challenges and the learning curves.

Wealth Concept

Do the most important things first.

The Wheel of Business is about identifying the pieces of your business that will need to be cultivated over time. Rome was not built in a day and neither is your business. It will be ever-changing and evolving.

At the age of 16, I was highly intrigued at the prospect of owning a business vs. being an employee.

Recently my 23-year-old son and I went out to dinner. Cameron said with absolute conviction, "I'll tell you one thing I know for sure. I am done ever working for anyone other than myself." I could not have been more proud. Knowing what works for you is the key to building a great business and career.

The Wheel of Business

This final wheel in our Wheel Trilogy is all about building the business that you need to create the life that you want. By using this wheel, you can start to not only understand what the key components of your business are, but you can begin to set goals against each of those components and help to ensure that you create exactly what you need. Understanding the Wheel of Business helps you to identify the areas where you need more attention and to set your business goals. You can plan your business over time to help support the success that you want.

WHEEL OF BUSINESS

Sales is the exchange of money for programs and products that teach and enrich our lives or our businesses. It is the exchange of something of value for something of greater value. And creates something that gives us satisfaction in life.

Sales is all about having the ability to work with your clients to help them understand the value of the product or program that you are providing.

Marketing is about your message. It's how you communicate the value of your products and services to your audience. The key to great marketing is to believe in yourself and have confidence in the value of the services that you provide to your customers.

Your marketing strategy includes the various ways that you communicate the value of your programs or products to your audience. It helps to make sure that you have enough fishing poles in the water.

Networking is simply talking to people. It is no longer enough to have a strong advertising or marketing campaign; you have to have a strong network.

Networking is building a community of people who you trust and who trust you. The people you spend time with the most will greatly influence the person you become. To truly become a successful entrepreneur, you need to spend time with other successful entrepreneurs and other successful people.

Self-care is taking care of your body, mind, spirit and creating the energy you need to do everything you need to do. You've heard the saying, "You can't pour from an empty cup." That is true more now than ever. On average, our lives are busier than ever before. We have enormous responsibilities. If you run a business your responsibilities are not only to yourself and your family, they are also to your team and your clients.

The best way to be able to take the best care of others is by taking the best care of yourself.

Self-care comes in many forms (we will explore this topic in more detail later in the book). The more you focus on taking care of you, the better you can be for everyone around you.

Relationships are the connections you are able to make with other people. Sales is all relationships. The way that you build your relationships can do a lot to help make your business successful.

There are many types of relationships that are important to your business. Your relationships with your team, your clients, your suppliers and your business partners are all critical to building a successful business.

Systems includes all of the processes that you put in place to ensure that your business is run in an efficient manner.

Your systems hold the key to making your business run with ease and grace. They help you avoid having to create new steps every time you bring on a new customer, create a new marketing campaign or build a new product. The more systems you have that help you run your business, the more time you will be able to spend building relationships and taking care of what is important.

Delegation is finding the right people to help you to fulfill all of your responsibilities. In order to truly create virtual wealth, you must become comfortable with others taking on part of your duties. The more you can delegate the activities that aren't as important, the more time you can spend on the important activities. You might begin with delegating some of your personal and administrative activities. I have very quickly gotten used to having someone else cook my meals, clean my space and send my emails. As your business grows and you become more comfortable, you will find it important to delegate more.

It is also important to remember that delegation is not always about you. As you are building a team, it is important to use delegation to help your team members be successful as well. Used in the right way, delegation can be an important training tool and can help to build trust and confidence in your team.

Wheel of Business exercise: Evaluating and Goal Setting

Use the exercise on the following page to build and assess your Wheel of Business. (Note: follow the same instructions as the Wheel of Life exercise.)

I suggest that you find a quiet place to go through this exercise. If you meditate, you might do a short meditation beforehand to help create a peaceful mindset and open yourself up to possibilities. Make sure you have at least 30 minutes to perform the exercise. Make sure you spend some time really considering what you have in your life and what you want in your life.

Step 1 - What you currently have in your life:

On a Scale of 1-6, indicate where you think you are in achieving your goals in each of these categories

1 = I am not achieving my goals, or I have not set any goals

6 = I am exactly where I want to be

1. Sales _____

2. Marketing _____

3. Networking _____

4. Self-Care _____

5. Relationships _____

6. Systems _____

7. Delegation _____

Now take a marker, crayon, pencil or anything you would like and fill in the wheel with your scores. If you'd like, make a copy of the page so that you can do the exercise again and see how you progress over time.

Step 2:

On the next page, define the goals that you would like to set for yourself for each item. Think about what you would like to have in 1 year, 3 years and 5 years.

Pay close attention to those items that you rated a 3 or less.

Virtual Wealth: Create Revenue & Amazing Relationships

	What I want in my life in the next year	What I want in my life in the next 3 years	What I want in my life in the next 5 years
Sales			
Marketing			
Networking			
Self Care			
Relationships			
Systems			
Delegation			

These goals are very important to the growth of your business. Spend time thinking about your goals. If you have a business coach, discuss your goals with your coach.

Create Your Business Plan

Now that you have identified the areas of your business that you want to focus on, you can now create your plan. Think about specific steps to take that will help you reach your goals. You want your plan to be actionable, realistic, measurable and timely. Don't think you need to plan out for the next 6 months. If you aren't a planner, think about the next week or two weeks. Write down 3-4 actions you can take in that timeframe and put them on your list.

Revisit your goals again every couple of weeks and identify 3-4 more activities that you can complete in the next couple of weeks. Continue to repeat every few weeks and you might be amazed at the difference you see.

For all of the *Wheel* exercises (Life, Fitness and Business), keep your goals in a place where you can pull them out periodically and review them. After about 6 months, you may find that you have made such progress in certain areas that it's time to fill the wheel in a little more. You might decide that it's time to set some new goals. With this focus, your wheel will improve and become more balanced over time and I think you will find your life and your business will become more balanced as well.

6 FIND JOY IN YOUR BUSINESS

"The happiest people don't have the best of everything, they just make the best of everything.

Zig Zigler,

Author and Motivational Speaker

Care was in his blood and in his being and it brought him a lot of joy. It also brought a lot of stress.

Chuck was a personal training client who made the most progress in the shortest amount of time. Chuck lived such an amazing life, but it was a life that many would have seen as full of challenges. Chuck was 200 pounds overweight when we came to me. He was running a home health service business as well as taking care of his elderly mother-in-law.

As we started working together to help him release the weight, his mother-in-law continued to have health challenges. Many people would have put their own health on hold to focus on their family. He knew that key to ensuring his business stayed healthy and his mother-in-law received the care she needed was to make sure that he was as healthy as he could be.

Over the course of 16 months, Chuck lost 200 pounds. As Chuck got healthier, so did his business. It became more successful and Chuck was able to provide his mother-in-law with the care that she needed.

As business owners and practitioners, it is easy to allow the stress of our business to take over our lives. In many cases, we allow it to get to the point that we lose the joy in the work and we become stuck.

Or, alternatively, we have stress happening in our personal lives that make our businesses challenging.

Events happen throughout our lives and the life of our business that are unexpected. A loss, an upsetting event, maybe even a catastrophic unforeseen event occurs. We are constantly being challenged with opportunities to grow. The way we face these challenges and opportunities is likely the reason we are sought out by our clients.

I have found over the years that there are times when I am moving ahead in my life and business and times where I may not be as productive as I'd like.

Wealth Concept

Today is the best day ever

I have always found inspiration in the concept of "<u>and</u> not <u>or</u>". This is one of the first lessons I learned as I was learning about life coaching. I can have a cookie *and* be fit and lean. I can build a business *and* deal with going through a divorce. I can be successful *and* park my emotional wounds while being highly productive. The concept of "<u>and</u> not <u>or</u>" is a game-changer in becoming highly strategic and emotionally resilient. You may never get over the death of a loved one, but you can live in gratitude for their love and life.

Communication is one of the key factors that tie in with this high level of functioning as we run our business and our lives. We have to be transparent and authentic in our communication all while maintaining healthy boundaries in our relationships. This specific combination makes for incredible working relationships.

You have to know when to give yourself permission to tap out, take a break or change directions. I call it "giving yourself grace and space." There will be times when we put the bigger projects and goals on hold or shift deadlines. It's really okay. Everything takes time and often it takes longer than we initially thought it would.

I have found a lot of success in approaching each day as if it's the best day ever. After all, it's the only one we've got. I ask myself, why can't every day have some elements of the joy, bliss and gratitude that happens during an incredible birthday, wedding, or winning a competition?

Wear the sparkle, buy the flowers, eat the cake, go on the adventure, take great pictures and use the expensive China for breakfast.

It's A Part of Me

The "A part of me" concept changed my life. I was getting stuck and holding on to emotions that got in the way of my productivity. I was on a client coaching call with Monica Shah the first time I heard of this and it changed my life. It turns out that a part of me can be upset while the whole of me lives in the knowingness that life is unfolding in ways we cannot predict.

What we did next really changed me. Monica asked me to sit down quietly and ask myself "What are you tolerating?"

Think about the last time you got upset and carried around an emotion (rightfully so) for a while. How long did you carry that story around and let it resonate with you?

It turned out I had been upset for a week after overhearing a phone conversation that said something negative about me. I was mad, hurt and upset for a full week. I carried that conversation around with me and it affected the other parts of my life and my work.

I have learned to let more go. I can be upset with something, but if I let that something control my next steps, I can't be the best for my business, my clients, my friend or my family.

Even when you are going through really big life challenges, you can be productive and have a sense of gratitude.

We make choices to embrace an emotional state and continue to think about it, talk about it and make it our reality moment by moment. Every time I really focus on "Today is the BEST DAY EVER" wonderful gifts appear.

Even though Chuck was working 7 days a week and cared for his dying mother-in-law in their home in hospice, he got his workouts and food log done. He lost 200 lbs. in 16 months while a part of him was under extreme duress and stress.

You have to want your outcomes more than you want to succumb to the stress and strain of life as it happens.

7 SELF-CARE IS NOT NEGOTIABLE

"The biggest difference between money and time is you always know how much money you have, but you never know how much time you have."

Unknown

Self-care can mean a lot of things to a lot of people. For some, it can mean spending a Saturday at a Spa or getting a massage. For others, it's taking a break from sugar as your go-to when you are stressed. It can mean taking a day off to take your kids to a museum or schedule a weekend away with your best friends or as simple as a date night with your significant other.

Most of us have stretches in our lives where we are not spending enough time with self-care and need to step up. You are not alone; we all go through times when we cannot or do not take care of ourselves.

Statistically, we are not healthy. I spent 25 years teaching "clean eating" and taught thousands of people to eat clean, exercise and have a healthy mindset with my Simple Fat Burn program. Meanwhile, sixty percent of us, or more, struggle with our weight and health issues that can be changed with nutrition, consistent exercise and mindset work.

Over the years, I have had many clients who adopted the clean eating and exercise approach who came back saying "I can't believe how good I feel..." Sometimes you don't even know how bad you feel until you start feeling better with healthy habits.

As a teenager, I read a book about weight loss. In my younger years, I had an extreme struggle with my weight. The author of that book posed the question: would you rather have a big diamond ring on a fat finger or a thin healthy finger with a small gold band? I thought for a moment and said to myself... I would like the thin healthy finger with both rings.

Somehow, we believe we can only have one wish when the genie shows up with her magical bottle. The truth is you can have as many wishes as you want.

Belief combined with action can bring many layers of manifestation in your life.

You can have what you want and the next bigger better thing too. You don't have to give up your social life and family time to run a successful business or have a successful corporate career.

You do have to protect your time, schedule and delegate. You really can have it all. What has to happen is skills, systems, boundaries, scheduling and you must have clarity about exactly how this is going to happen. Write it down. The power of the written word is critical. Listen to what you are saying to yourself about your situation. If something is not going well, talk to a trusted friend or a professional. A little insight and help go a long way.

Your Morning Routine

A consistent morning routine can become a big part of your self-care strategy. A morning routine doesn't have to be complicated, but it can help get your mind moving in the right direction every day.

My morning routine consists of three elements Mind – Spirit – Body

For me, I start every day with 10 to 15 minutes of meditation. It calms my mind and gets me ready to start the day. If you aren't sure how to get started with meditation, don't think it has to be difficult. There are lots of internet videos on meditation as well as several apps that you can use to help you get started. Start slow – maybe 5-10 minutes. I think you will find it's a great way to get your mind calm and ready for whatever challenges and joys you have during your day.

Next, I spend a few minutes scripting. Scripting is a type of journaling that you can read more about later in the book in the Scripting chapter. Scripting helps me to be thoughtful about my upcoming day and set my intentions for the day. I use the time to think about what I have on my schedule and how I can make the most of my time for myself and for my clients. It also helps me think forward to set intentions for the week, month and future so that I can help to ensure that all of my actions are benefiting not only my now but my future self.

My third step for the morning is exercise. I usually try to get outside for a few minutes during my exercise time or to the gym. My exercise routine can be as strenuous as taking a run or doing some strength training or it can be as light as a good brisk walk and some stretching. I have found that making an effort to intentionally move my body every day helps my mind focus on the important work that I have to get done every day.

The other daily routine that I have is taking advantage of my community pool. Not only does it give me time to relax, I get my daily dose of sunshine and vitamin D and perhaps get to run into one of my sweet neighbors.

Self-Care Action Plan

Here's a quick activity you can do to help you build a daily routine for self-care.

For this exercise you will need paper, pen/pencil/marker, notecards and a timer (the timer on your phone will work fine)

Note: I always recommend that before you start any brainstorming exercise that you take a couple of minutes to close your eyes and take a couple of deep breaths. This helps to ground you and focus your mind. Also perform any other ritual that helps you to process and be creative (light a candle, say a prayer, burn some incense).

1. Grab a piece of paper and a pen/pencil/marker

2. Set a timer for 5-10 minutes

3. Think about as many activities you can perform that will promote your self-care and write them down.

4. Keep writing until your timer goes off.

5. Capture each activity that you identified on a notecard.

Now, you have a tool that will help you to create self-care any time during any day. Keep these cards in a place where you can easily access them. When you have few minutes during your day, pull a card and you now have an action you can take to take care of yourself.

Take note: These do not all have to be quick activities. Be sure to set aside time for big stuff too – a weekend away, travel, a day spent with your family, date night, a two week vacation.

Some Self-Care Ideas

Just in case you're struggling to come up with self-care ideas, here are a few keywords that might help with your brainstorming.

8 CONNECT WITH YOUR IDEAL CUSTOMER: WHAT'S IN IT FOR ME

"The first step towards getting somewhere is to decide you're not going to stay where you are."

John Pierpont Morgan,

Financier

Have you ever asked yourself "What's in it for me?" The first time I heard of the WIIFM concept I was reading a book by Neale Donald Walsch. He wrote about the concept that "everyone is in everything for themselves" I was blown away by this concept. It seemed to explain everything I needed to know about how to really connect with others. Every human being has a motive, a payoff for every action they take. Some of those actions are entirely self-serving and many do serve the greater good.

Wealth Concept

Do the most important things first.

This is a critical concept to understand human behavior, growing a network, sales and marketing. Once I began to fully understand, it changed the way I began interacting with everyone.

It changed my communications and marketing.

It changed how to conducted my sales conversations

Most importantly, it changed how I saw myself as a leader, helper and server to not only my clients but to my entire community.

The WIIFM concept for me is all about helping me to become more serving to everyone around me. When I have a conversation with a prospective client, I can now turn the conversation more to them and their needs. The conversation is no longer about my programs and services, it becomes about what my clients need. What they are struggling with? What keeps them up at night?

I listen. I offer advice. I offer help. I do not sell. I use the time to build my relationship with them and learn about who they are as people.

I have a number of entrepreneur friends who have sales conversations with prospective clients. To me, those conversations are not sales conversations. For me, they are connection conversations.

I may not close a sale in that first conversation. But I know I am building a lasting relationship and when the time is right, I will build a business relationship with that person.

9 BECOME THE ARCHITECT OF YOUR BUSINESS

"Everything I do is based on ROI"

Deborah Daniel,

CPA Charter Accounting

The concept of virtual wealth is all about creating a business that supports your personal goals. If you want to live on an island, you can create a business that supports that. If you want to be able to spend your days exploring the museums of Europe, you can build a business that supports that. And you can build a business that helps you to spend time with your family and friends.

It's also about creating and living your legacy. The people you help become your cheerleaders, your advocates and your biggest fans. They in turn can spread what you create to others.

You have the ability to create exactly the business that you need to create the life you want.

One of the first steps to building the business that you want is to understand exactly what you want that business to be and what lifestyle you want to build it around.

Wealth Concept

People don't buy programs and products...they buy freedom and emotional experiences

Once you understand what you want to build in your life and your business, you need to determine exactly what you want to provide in your business. What are the programs, products and services that you want and need to provide to your clients? Do those programs, products and services serve you and your goals for your life and your business?

Most of our clients are looking for solutions to their problems.

A new business owner needs advice on how to get more clients.

A massage client needs relief from pain

A young couple needs to get out of debt

A busy practitioner has reached their ceiling and needs to be able to serve more clients.

People don't buy programs and products...they buy freedom and emotional experiences

Keep remembering the above statement. People are looking for ways to make their lives easier. They are looking for ways to create better experiences for themselves. When you can answer those deepest questions that your clients have, your business can grow exponentially.

Wealth anchoring exercise:

It is important for you to understand how your clients feel about purchasing your services. One of the best ways to do that is to put yourself in their shoes. Use the following exercise to help you picture and feel as your customers might be thinking and feeling.

Think of one of your happiest, greatest purchases. Maybe it was a program you invested in that absolutely changed your life for the better. Maybe it was a car, a trip, your beach house, or a dating site that brought you love.

I bought

_____

_____

The value I got was

_____

_____

I felt

_____

_____

You might now spend some time journaling about what you discovered during the above exercise.

Now, put yourself in the place of your customer. Think about your ideal customer. Answer the questions from the exercise above through the eyes of your ideal customer.

Did you capture similar comments? What was different? Is there anything you think you need to change about your products or programs based on what you captured?

You can use this information to think about what you might need to change about your programs in order to begin to better reach your ideal client.

Your Business Plan

Your business plan will help you to define what your business is, how you help your clients and how you support your mission. It is important to have your business plan documented so that you can review it often.

If you aren't sure what you need to include in your business plan, include your Vision Statement, Mission Statement, Values, Program Names and Descriptions, and a description of your Ideal Client. Read below for more information on each of these components.

Vision Statement

Your Vision Statement is a description of the aspirations of what you want your business to become.

Here are a few examples:

Nike: Bring inspiration and innovation to every athlete* in the world (*If you have a body, you are an athlete).

LinkedIn: Create economic opportunity to every member of the global workforce.

San Diego Zoo: To become a world leader at connecting people to wildlife and conservation.

Your Vision Statement helps you to define and communicate to your ideal client where you are going so, they can be motivated to go with you.

Mission Statement

The mission statement is a statement of how you will reach your vision. It is action-oriented and may include specific steps that you will take.

Take the Nike Vision Statement above, their mission statement is:

"Create groundbreaking sports innovations, make our products sustainably, build a creative and diverse global team, and make a positive impact on communities where we live and work."

This mission statement includes specific things that will be put in place by Nike to ensure that they are about to realize their vision.

The Mission Statement is more about taking action. It's about what you are doing or will do to create the vision you want for your life and your business.

Values

Your values – or code of ethics – define who you are and what you want your business to be. Your values help you to know how you interact with others (clients, suppliers and employees), and provides a moral direction for your business. Your values statement helps you to define the heart of your company.

Some examples of values may include:

- Teamwork

- Integrity

- Authenticity

- Customer Focused

- Kind

- Diversity

- Quality

Your Values are a reflection of the type of business you want to have and how you want it to operate in this world. They help create a connection with your clients and help them to see that you are exactly the right person and this is the right business.

Program Names and Descriptions

Use your business plan to document the name and description of each program. Include the benefits, features and pricing. Also, be sure to document what flexibility you have in any of the pricing (e.g., payment plan options, sliding scale options, etc.)

Ideal Client Description

By writing a description of your ideal client, you can create a very clear picture of anyone with whom you want to work. You may take the opportunity to write more than one description in order to ensure that you create some flexibility.

You may choose to add more elements to your business plan. The purpose of the business plan is to make sure you have in writing what you want to build. Include anything else that helps you to describe that.

Don't forget to review your plan often – I would recommend weekly. If your life or your goals start to change, it's completely acceptable to adjust your plan with the changes.

10 CREATE REVENUE WITH EASE

"Money Loves Clarity"

Monica Shah,

Business Coach and Author

You are not a car salesman. For the typical car salesman, their strategy is to make you tired, keep you on the sales floor for a long time, allow your blood sugar to drop so you can't think as well. They use those physical weaknesses to overwhelm you and make a decision without having a clear head.

You are not that. You care about your clients and want to make sure they get what they need.

For most of us, the biggest struggle we have with sales is that we get into our own heads and get in our own way. We allow the stories that we tell ourselves to convince us that we can't do it and fight the natural abilities that we have.

You have a unique mission and talents that can help others. One of the first steps is to understand your mission and what you do best to help your clients.

I always approach sales from a heart-centered, serving place. I have found that by making a connection with my clients and showing them that I truly care about them, I have grown my business exponentially. This also allows me the chance to work with the most amazing people.

The Connection Conversation

The connection conversation is all about getting to know your potential client and allowing them to get to know you. It's about offering help and serving. You may use this connection to begin to educate your prospect on your products or programs. If this is your right and perfect client, you may not have a sales conversation at this point.

At this point, you may choose to not talk about pricing. You want to get to know your client first. In your conversation, you may uncover what's going on in their lives. What their struggles are and how they are overcoming them.

You may also find information that will help you to understand how you can help them. It's not about a sales conversation. It's just about building a relationship and understanding who and where they are in their lives and business.

Talking Price

Creating sales in your business is all about your mission. You have to believe in what you are doing to help people and approach your sales from the heart.

Many entrepreneurs spend their time over-thinking the price. When we should all be working to ensure that we are providing value.

Approach your prospective client as a person and make sure that what you are giving them meets their needs. If you help them to truly understand what your program or product can do to help them, you will find your perfect client. Once you find your perfect clients, price won't matter.

Sales is all about building relationships. As the relationship is unfolding, they get to know you and you get to know them. Trust is built with every conversation.

What's more, if you create your sales based on relationships, creating value and giving your clients exactly what they need, you create more confidence in yourself and are able to deliver a better experience for your clients.

Before you know it you are able to double or triple the price of your programs and create sales with ease. You create happy clients and you become more satisfied with your work.

Find the Right Clients for You

Everyone has a different communication method that works for them. Some primarily communicate through email, some through text, many like to get information through social media and others prefer the personalized touch of a phone call. I have found that when I use all of the communication vehicles, I can find the right way to build those important relationships.

I have even built relationships with people by having them overhear a conversation during one of my connection meetings.

The communication method is not what matters. What matters is your ability to be an active listener who demonstrates empathy and understanding.

Wealth Concept

How many times do you follow up?

Until they buy from you.

The number one skill that you can learn that will make the biggest difference in your business is empathy. Your ability to honor where someone is and help them to through their own process can speak volumes and build trust in the relationship as quickly as almost anything you can do.

How do you operate with empathy and build your client base?

"I will do anything I can to help you." Honor where they are and do anything to help them through their process.

Be willing to offer something for free – give them a book or an article or something else that might help them. You never know who's going to come back through the door down the road.

Select your clients – pre-qualified with Time, Money and Interest. Get to know them so well that you know: Are they really interested? Are they really committed? Do they really have the funds to support this venture? Are they the right fit for me, my program, my values?

I don't work with people who do not fit the culture of what I believe in. There is nothing wrong with saying no; don't be afraid of no. You can support someone and make recommendations to someone who might not fit. You might even have someone else in your network who could be a better fit and in return help that other person as well.

I have found that the entrepreneurs who struggle the most are those who choose clients that are not the right fit or don't align with their values.

Wealth Concept

Communication is about an outcome

Knowing Your Worth and Making Your Offer

There will come a time in every relationship with a potential client that you will have to be prepared to set your price for your program. The best way that you can show your value and ensure that you get what you are worth is to have everything written down.

The anatomy of your offer includes 5 critical components:

Problem - Solution - Benefits - Features - Action

The Problem

This is the wake-up-in-the-morning problem for your client. Remember the three reasons people buy are Health, Wealth and Relationships. They want better health, more money and better relationships and are willing to pay for those.

The Solution

Your program or product will help your client to improve at least one of those three components. You will need to be able to show your prospective clients that you have the solution for that problem. This is one reason that you have to start with the conversation. Your conversations will help you to understand the wake-up-in-the-morning problem. They will also help you to be able to explain how your program will solve that problem.

The Benefits

The benefits include an explanation of how the specifics of the program will help the prospective client. For instance, with my Virtual Health program, one of the benefits is that I teach my clients how to manage their insulin levels in order to burn fat including what foods to eat or not to eat. I also teach my clients how to measure the right numbers so that they know how they are doing on a day-to-day basis. These are benefits that other similar programs might not offer.

The Features

The features of the program describe how the program or offer might work. I might offer a prospective client a VIP session at the beginning of the program in order to develop their plan. Or, I my offer a d particular program that includes 12 sessions over 6 months with a monthly Q&A session. This is the information that you will share with your clients to help ensure that they understand not only what they will be getting with the offer, but also understand the boundaries.

The Action

This is the action that you need the prospective client to take in order to opt into the program. Maybe you need that person to sign-up via a website or call you directly. If the client doesn't know what step to take, they might not have the confidence to approach you directly. It is important that you are crystal clear on what you need them to do to sign up for your program or purchase your product. Otherwise, they may walk out of the room and move on to the next product.

The key to a great sales conversation and offer is that everyone comes away from the experience feeling good about the outcome.

Remember, you are not a car salesman!

11 START SMALL VIRTUALLY, THEN GROW BIG

Stick to your true north – build greatness for the long term

Ruth Porat,

CFO, Alphabet

Most purchases are motivated by freedom and emotions.

We and our clients are willing to invest in products and programs that promise to improve our Health, bring us better Relationships and increase our Income. Most people are looking for solutions to their problems and will buy when they feel they have found those solutions.

Wealth Concept
Money is the Ultimate Exchange of Value

Most of our clients are drawn to us because they are struggling with something and they are looking for a solution.

Not every business can be virtual. When I had my painting business, I would not have been able to create a virtual business. You can't create a virtual plumbing business or be a virtual house builder. During my career as a personal trainer, I thought I didn't have the opportunity to create a virtual business. I had to be in person for all of my clients.

At the height of my personal training business, I saw 25 to 30 clients a day. All of them in person. At the end of the day, I found myself exhausted. I love each and every one of my clients, but working from 5:30 am to 6:00 pm most days left me very tired.

I thought that in order to serve my clients, I had to see them in person. I had to be with them so that I could show them what to do and talk to them face to face. I needed to be with them to build the strong relationships.

Then I met Alice.

Alice was retired and needed to get healthier. She didn't have the time or the ability to meet with me in person every week. What's more, she didn't have the desire to fit into that same mold. She came to me through a referral and what she needed was some advice, some guidance and a plan.

I wrote out a meal plan and an exercise plan for her and she paid me for this plan. This was my first true virtual client. I didn't have to schedule her into my weekly schedule. I didn't have to see her at 6:00 in the morning.

Alice motivated me to find different ways to run my business. It would be several years before I had a truly virtual business, but she helped me realize that there were other possibilities.

Income Types

One of the best ways to understand how virtual wealth can work for you is to understand the three different types of income that you can earn as an entrepreneur, business owner or professional

Baseline Income

Baseline income is typically exchanging hours for dollars. It's a job or a business in which you exchange time for an hourly fee or a salary. For many people, this is their corporate job or their primary business. For me, for many years, it was my personal training business. I charged an hourly rate for all of my clients.

Topline Income

Topline income is the next level of business where you create programs or products. This type of income is about exchanging value for revenue.

Typically, these programs are set up in a way that you receive monthly subscription payments or your clients pay for 6 or 12 months for a program. This allows you to control what income is coming in based on the value you provide to your clients.

When you deliver programs to your clients, you can drive more revenue by charging higher fees for serving many people at once (group programs).

Empire income

Empire income is created when you begin to significantly scale your business and is the highest level of income in virtual wealth. Empire income can bring you exponentially higher rates for your expertise with your VIP services. Typically, these are large offers to groups or individuals. This type of income can also be realized through selling from the stage, creating large group programs and creating automated sales.

As with Top Line income, your revenue can be generated through subscriptions to memberships and programs.

Once you start to create empire income, you can begin to realize the lifestyle that true virtual wealth can bring you.

Sales to Start Small Virtually

The key is starting in a way that allows you to be successful.

Start with the easiest thing to sell.

Price it appropriately.

Make sure it's something that has value so you can overdeliver on value.

If you price your program so high when you are starting off, you may become uncomfortable with asking for that price. If it's priced right, you will be more confident with your conversations and can ask for the sale much more easily.

I struggled with this myself in my first online coaching group. I had been a personal trainer for more than 20 years and I was beginning to explore virtual programs. My business coach told me that I should sell the program at $495 per month.

I didn't have the confidence to ask for that monthly rate from my clients. I was, however, comfortable with a rate of $250. I was able to confidently ask for that amount and built a program with 10 people right away. I was also able to over-deliver to my clients and continue to build my confidence so that I could ask for a higher rate in my next program.

Within 6 months, I was able to sell the same program for double then triple from what I started. As I raised my rates, my container expanded and I was able to deliver even more to my clients.

12 You Are the Best Marketer I Know

"You don't have to be great to start, but you have to start to be great."

Zig Ziglar,

Speaker and Writer

Marketing is all about communications. And communications are really about talking to people in any way you can – through email, phone, text, social media. Any way you can find to get to your perfect clients is the right way.

I have a friend who I met after she participated in one of my free workshops. It has been several years since we first met, but we stayed connected through social media and mutual friends, but we hadn't had the deep personal connection yet.

One evening I was dining with friends and Victoria was at the same restaurant with a mutual friend of ours. That mutual friend brought her over to introduce us which started a very strong connection between the two of us.

We started having regular conversations and I reached out to her a number of times to offer any help I could. She didn't become a client right away, but I continued to stay connected.

Then one day while we were chatting, she started to ask about my programs and wanted to know more. After a couple more conversations, we both decided the time was right for us to begin working together.

Every conversation we had was part of my marketing approach. I used every conversation, every contact, every reach out to help her learn more about me, my business and my programs. Once she felt comfortable and she knew I was a person she could trust, she became my client – and has now become one of my most successful clients.

Know Your Market

One of the most important steps to building your marketing plan is defining your target market. You need to be able to picture who you are marketing to. You need to understand what they care about, what keeps them up at night and what they love.

Make you know spend some time understanding your market by asking yourself the following questions.

How old are they?

What do they do for work?

Are they male or female?

What are their hobbies?

Are they married? Do they have children?

Where do they live?

Where do they vacation?

What is their wake-up in the morning problem?

If you are creative or like to draw, you might even create a picture of what your ideal client looks like. You can also give her or him a name.

When you are creating your marketing content, use this information to create an image in mind about who you are targeting, who you are creating the content for. Write your content as if you are talking directly to that person.

Once you understand who your clients are, then you can start serving them. It's about being visible and making sure people know who you are and how you can help them. Great marketing is about serving not selling.

Be a listener. Show empathy. You cannot be empathetic if you do not listen to what your clients are saying. Honor where someone is and help them do anything to help them through their process.

It's not about a sales conversation. It's just about a conversation, building a relationship, understanding where they are.

Remember, you can select your clients – pre-qualified with time, money and interest. I always make sure that my clients fit my culture. If they don't, we will both struggle with the relationship. Don't be afraid to say no. If people don't love their clients, they can struggle in their business.

If you believe they are the right person for you and your business, you will know it in your gut. Anything you do to help them will be the valuable to both you and the client, even if it's just your time.

You want everyone to come away from the experience feeling good about the outcome – including you.

Reach Your Ideal Client

I think of marketing as putting as many fishing poles in the water as you can. There are many ways to reach your clients and I encourage you to use as many of them as you can. Try as many of the different methods if you would like. Use the ones that work and discard those that don't.

The 30-day Marketing Challenge.

I suggest starting at the beginning of each month to make it easier to track your 30-day challenge. Every day in that 30 days spend time on one of the following marketing activities:

Create a website and find ways to drive people to your site

Create a social media group

Facebook lives

Posting to all of your social media accounts

Finding speaking events

Networking events

Facebook Ads

Emails to customers or potential customers

Newsletters to your contacts

Writing a blog or video post

Create a Podcast

Pay attention to what other successful people are using to communicate about their business and try those methods as well. If one doesn't work, it's not a failure, it's simply a way to learn what does and does not work for you.

Wealth Concept

Be visible and go where your people are. Let them know what you are really good at.

High Vibrational Words

When it comes to your marketing, words matter. Using the right words in your message can raise someone's energy and reach them at a subconscious level. I always focus on using high vibrational words. These are words that create energy, optimism, confidence and attraction.

This is a very different concept than the traditional marketing strategy of creating FUD - Fear, Uncertainty and Doubt.

On the next page is a sampling of some High-Vibration words. Review the list and see what others you can think of. Begin finding ways to use these words in your communications with others and see the difference that it makes.

Ability | Abundance | Acceptance | Achievement
Affirming | Alertness | Amazement | Ascendency
Ascension | Assistance | Authenticity | Awareness | Beauty
Benevolence | Blessings | Bliss   Bounty | Calmness
Celebration | Certainty | Comfort | Concentration   Cosmic
| Courage | Courtesy | Creativity | Decency   Delight |
Desire | Ease | Ecstasy | Elegance | Endearment Endeavor
| Endurance | Energized | Energy | Enhancement Enjoyment
| Enlightenment | Enough | Enrichment   Equality | Esteem
| Ethics | Expertise | Faith Fellowship   Forgiveness |
Freedom | Fulfillment | Fun | Generosity   Gentleness |
Genuine | Giving | Glorious | Goodness   Grace | Gratitude
| Guidance | Happy | Health   Helpfulness | Honesty |
Hope | Incredible | Innocence   Integrity | Intelligence |
Involvement | Joy | Kindness   Laughter | Lavishness |
Liberation | Life | Light | Liking   Listening | Love |
Love of Life | Loyalty Luck | Lucrative   Luxuriant |
Magnificence | Manifesting | Marvelous   Mediation | Mercy
| Merit | Miracles | Money   Motivation | New | Nirvana
| Noticeable | Nourished   Open-Minded | Optimism |
Order | Originality | Outgoing   Paradise | Patience |
Peace | Plenty | Polite | Potentials   Power | Preciousness |
Productivity | Proficiency | Promotion   Punctuality |
Purpose | Quantum | Quietness | Readiness   Reassurance |
Refreshment | Release | Respect | Responsibility
Restoration | Reward | Rich | Safe | Satisfaction | Self-
Assertive | Self-Control | Self-Love | Simplicity | Sobriety |
Special   Spectacular | Spirit | Success | Sufficient
Sympathy | Tact   Thanks | Thrive | Timeliness | Tolerance
| Tranquility   Triumphant | Trust | Truthfulness | Upbeat
| Uplifted   Upstanding | Valuable | Versatile | Vibrant |
Virtuous   Vitality | Warmth | Welcome | Wholesome |
Will | Win   Wisdom | Wonderful

13
CREATE YOUR IDEAL RELATIONSHIPS

"Surround yourself with those who see greatness within you,

even when you don't see it yourself."

Zig Ziglar,

Speaker, Writer, Motivator

You never know where learning and inspiration might appear. A few years ago, I was traveling across the country. I was in the mountains of Virginia and I found an area where I decided to spend the night. My hotel was near a small shopping center and there was an Outback Steakhouse in that area where I went to get a bite to eat.

I got to the restaurant and there were lots of cars in the parking lot and there was a waitlist to get in to get a table. It made me curious about why this restaurant was so popular, especially when so many other restaurants were empty.

I got a table and was enjoying my dinner and a glass of wine. Then, I asked my server if I could get a half glass of wine. I didn't really want another full glass. She said, "no, we really don't do that."

I was finishing my dinner when a few minutes later the manager came over to check on me. I took the opportunity to ask him why this place was so busy. I got the most interesting answer.

He explained to me that he had worked for Outback for 19 years and they are so good to their people. He said, "I can't imagine doing anything besides being a manager for Outback. If I have someone I have trained and they don't work at my store anymore, I go to the other Outback and I think 'there's my Megan.'" He explained to me that it was the relationships that they have to influence the quality of the people they attract.

Then he said, "Oh, by the way, I am going to make that happen and get you that glass of wine on me."

I was so impressed with the customer service, his enthusiasm and the fact that he loved what he did and the people he did it with. I have never met a restaurant manager who was so enthusiastic about his job, the people and he just couldn't imagine working anywhere else.

Clearly, they are doing something also at the corporate level that influences that behavior. It's the culture. When people join the company, they don't want to leave.

If you have ever been in an Outback, they typically kneel down and talk with you at eye level or sit down with you and take your order. They are constantly building relationships with their customer. They make you feel very welcome and very appreciated.

This manager came to the table twice that evening to check on me. The entire wait staff was attentive and went out of their way to take care of their guests. The place was packed and the service was impeccable.

You can create the kind of relationship that not only allows you to build your own wealth but ensures that everyone in the relationship wins.

John Maxwell has a great quote: "Don't send your ducks to eagle school and don't send your eagles to duck school."

This is such a great concept. You want to recognize where each person is in their journey. Some people are ducks. They enjoy paddling around the lake. They fly when they need to move to a warmer climate, but mostly they are satisfied with their lake.

Eagles, on the other hand, are constantly moving. They love to soar. They fly high and take challenges. They are hunters and explorers.

If you try to send your ducks to eagle school, they will struggle. They can't soar like the eagles do. They can't dive down and capture their prey like eagles do. A duck can only be a duck. They cannot become an eagle.

During your journey through life and through your business, you will meet a lot of ducks and you will meet a lot of eagles. In building your relationships, it will be important for you to understand where your people are. Whether you are managing a team, working with your clients or meeting prospects, understanding people from their perspective will lead you to much success.

Years ago, I met John at a networking event. My conversation with John changed my perspective and really changed my life. We had a coffee appointment and everything he said made me LEAN IN and find him to be the most interesting and likable guy I'd met in a long time. There was really nothing special or notable about him at first glance. He was married with 4 kids. He was working on a goal of 20K per month in sales and was darn close to making it.

John and his wife took weekends and Mondays off and home-schooled four young kids.

They had their priorities in order and he was crystal clear about stating what their priorities were. God. Family. Friends. Work.

I asked him about his education, background and training. He said that his main influencer was a specific book that he had read 5 times and studied it. What in the world book could it be?!

It was an old Dale Carnegie book, *How To Win Friends And Influence People*. I'd actually read it years before and after that conversation with John, I decided to reread it.

That's how John made me hinge on every word he said. I got the book. Read it and realized I was already doing 90% of everything in the book. Perhaps that's why my business kept growing. I was winning sales contests and had 16 Personal trainers working for me. A lot of people would hear that I had 16 trainers that I managed and think how wildly successful that was. I was working soooo hard though. Having others for who you are responsible is difficult. It is hard dealing with all of those personalities and making sure everyone had the opportunity to be successful. And through it all, I still had strained relationships that I was wrestling with myself.

How to Win Friends and Influence People is all about Emotional Intelligence (EQ).

The key to understanding EQ - the emotional quotient, is empathy, having great listening skills, figuring out what people want (WIFM) and then really helping them get it. This is a huge concept in terms of building wealth. Why? People are your connection. They will open the doors to the clients, customers, resources, systems and everything nice in life!

Use Your Network to Build Your Network

Whether you realize it or not, we all have a network or a circle. These are the people who mean the most to us. They are our family and friends and the people we spend our time with – colleagues or co-workers, people from our social circle, people who attend the same functions that we attend (church, clubs, organizations), etc.

Don't be afraid to ask for help. Let your network know what you are looking for, and your perfect client description. Ask for introductions to people they know who you want to get to know.

If your network doesn't know your business or your story, share it with them. Help them to understand why they should introduce their friends, family and network to you.

Know Where Your People Are and Go There

One of the keys to building the right relationships for your business is to know where to find the right people who either need your products or services or know the people who do.

A couple of years ago, I joined a private club. That has been one of the best decisions of my life. It has really upped my game in my relationships. I have found that I have been able to meet not only great people who have become clients, but I have made so many great connections who are connecting me to the right people.

Your people may be at networking events, or conferences or at women's groups. You may have the ability to meet your perfect client when you are having coffee in a café or on social media. The point is to understand where they are and show up consistently.

I didn't create those powerful relationships by only being at the club for dinner once a month. I attend several events a month. I show up during the day and work from the club. I invite clients to meet me at the club. I put myself there so that I have every opportunity to meet and network with just the right people.

The key is showing up and allowing them to get to know the amazing person that you are.

Don't Be Afraid to Tell Your Story

People build trust with those who they know. Once you allow someone to understand the struggles that you have faced, how you have overcome those struggles and how you help others do the same, they will begin to understand how you can help them. People make connections through stories.

Even if the person you have talked to has never been through what you have, they will see part of themselves in your story and that will help you to make a stronger connection.

Telling your story takes some vulnerability and trust on your part as well. It tells your audience that you trust them with the information you are sharing and that you trust them to not judge you.

When you are honest and approach it with depth and meaning, there is no more powerful way to make a connection.

14

SCRIPT FOR YOUR FUTURE

"Give something every day."

Dr. Joyce Rennolds,

Motivator 1 to 1,000

I've been living these principles in every way possible. Not only have I taught the power of "I AM" statements. I live them every day. I write them down almost every day. My belief in the power of words has literally created the good, challenging and amazing circumstances in every area of life.

Karma has a way of unfolding in your life. Pointing one finger at someone leaves you with three fingers pointing back at yourself. Those three fingers represent thoughts, feelings and actions. Often the subconscious is the one creating those circumstances, patterns and stories.

I am a big believer in getting into the subconscious on a daily basis. Whatever ways work for you will exponentially manifest your desires.

We all have very powerful belief systems at work that create the manifestation process and draw things to us.

The concept and practice of scripting have profoundly changed my life. I owe all the credit and thanks to Dr. Joyce Rennolds, "Motivator of one or a Thousand", and author of "The Energy Connection", for teaching the concept of scripting. I met Joyce while speaking at an event we hosted called "Total Woman Makeover." Joyce taught the power of writing your new story. She taught me to script, and I've been doing this daily for several years.

Scripting gives a powerful perspective on keeping a journal. The results that I, and thousands of others, have experienced from scripting have been absolutely outstanding. The scripting process is specific. You get a journal, a really nice journal, to use as your scripting book. This is important, as it is a reflection of your life that you are actively creating. You dedicate the journal to yourself and add in some specific details about what you value in this process.

In your journal you create the new story of your life, keeping the writing in the present tense, and writing as if it has already happened. It is important to write about what you are thankful for, express appreciation, and keep the content positive.

Scripting in specific detail works best. You are in fact, creating your new life as you write. You are scripting "new" desires, dreams, scenarios and your reality. Scripting is an action that results in manifestation. You will find that the words you write show up in your life! I cannot express strongly enough the power of scripting.

This is such a simple practice that makes a massive difference in your health, relationships, finances, and every facet of life that you choose to focus on. Scripting is powerful and literally one of the best practices that I recommend engaging with on a daily basis. Script yourself lean, fit and incredibly healthy, amongst anything else your heart desires.

Here's an example:

Thank you for my extreme focus. I have clarity in my vision and purpose. My body is lean, toned, healthy and fit. My meals are healthy and balanced. I exercise daily and my results materialize with ease!

You can script for many things in life. In this context, we apply scripting to health, fitness and body fat loss. You may script to be a specific size, weight, body fat percentage and/or toned areas of your body.

Another example:

You can script for more peace, joy and love in your work, and in your life.

My mind is clear and focused. I easily find the right and perfect clients. Money comes to me with ease. I am confident in my ability to serve my clients and my business. My work brings joy to me, my team and my clients. I am deeply satisfied with my work and my life.

The more you script the more you will see this positive energy help to manifest what you desire and need.

16 LIVING IN GRACE

"GRACE means that all of your mistakes now serve a purpose instead of serving shame."

Brene Brown,

Researcher, Author

There are many definitions of Grace. Some include:

"Elegance or refinement"

"Courteousness or goodwill"

"Doing honor or credit to someone by one's presence"

I think of grace as flow. I love the idea of being in the flow of life. To live in a Godly state and in a state of being fully present and quick to forgive. It's just a beautiful place to live. When everything in my world is flowing and gracefully, it makes me feel lighter and more open.

In life and business, it is very easy to get caught up in ego and start doing battle with yourself when something is not going well. But, if you are coming from a place of living in grace, you see things for what they are. You can be more proactive instead of being reactive. You can literally begin to function in a different way than most people.

When you get your mind in a state of grace and being gracious and grateful, you can be very strategic and very positive about your life and your business. It begins to open up tremendous opportunities for you and begins to wash away the self-doubt and struggles that you have with yourself.

By living in grace, you can start to look for the best outcomes for everyone involved no matter the situation.

If you are going to really enjoy your life and your business, finding grace is necessary.

Your "I Am" statements are very important here.

"I am grateful"

"I am gracious"

"I am forgiving"

"I am trusting"

When you get into the place of knowing that you can attract all of the right and perfect people into your network and as your customers, you create the ability to build new, powerful relationships and friendships.

It is really important to look and listen for signs of cultivating those relationships and keeping yourself grounded and focused. You can create a world where you are living in this place and space that other people want to be a part of. They will want to have more of what you have.

This doesn't mean that you will become perfect. It doesn't mean that you won't have your challenges. It does mean that you are stronger and more aligned than you may have been in the past. When you are living in grace, you are prepared for what challenges show up. Grace gives you the tools and the resources to be able to handle those challenges.

Made in the USA
Columbia, SC
06 July 2021

41464196R00075